ALL NEW

THE CAVAN JOKE
^ BOOK

G000163121

ALL NEW
THE CAVAN JOKE BOOK

Des MacHale

MERCIER PRESS
IRISH PUBLISHER – IRISH STORY

MERCIER PRESS

Cork

www.mercierpress.ie

© Des MacHale, 2012

ISBN: 978 1 85635 968 9

10 9 8 7 6 5 4 3 2 1

A CIP record for this title is available from the British Library

Printed and bound in the EU.

INTRODUCTION

Yes folks, here it is at last, *The All New Cavan Joke Book*. These jokes have proved very popular in Monaghan, Fermanagh, Leitrim, Longford and Meath and all over Ireland, but strangely enough not in Cavan itself!

I have now written joke books featuring Kerry men, Cork men, Mayo men, Dubliners, Cavan men, Englishmen and even Scotsmen. Who knows where the fickle finger of fun may land next? I am glad to say I have never received a letter of protest from a Cavan man concerning my joke books – well, stamps are expensive! On the other hand, if we all followed the financial carefulness practised by Cavan men, maybe we wouldn't be in the current crisis that we find ourselves in due to reckless overspending. I honestly believe that the only way forward is to literally laugh our way out of this recession. So enjoy and laugh yourself into happier times.

Des MacHale
Cork

To Doctor Niall Toibin,
the man who started it all off,
this book is affectionately dedicated.

Why is the population of Cavan so small?

Cavan men hate to part with anything!

☺   ☺   ☺

A Cavan man asked his wife what she wanted for her birthday.

'I'll give you a clue,' she told him. 'I can make it go from 0 to 150 in three seconds.'

So he bought her some weighing scales.

☺   ☺   ☺

A fellow called at a Cavan man's door collecting for the Old Folks' Home. So the Cavan man donated his grandparents.

☺   ☺   ☺

How do you recognise a Cavan motorist?

He turns off his windscreen wipers when he goes under a bridge.

☺   ☺   ☺

A Cavan man was teaching his dog to beg. And it paid off – last week the dog came home with €5.

☺   ☺   ☺

Why do Cavan men have long noses?

Fresh air is free.

☺   ☺   ☺

A Cavan man was praising his wife on the silver anniversary of their wedding.

'She has stood by my side since the day we were married,' he said proudly, 'but then, we had only one chair in the house.'

☺ ☺ ☺

A Cavan man was showing his friend his beautiful new watch.

'Fantastic,' said the friend, 'how did you come by it?'

'My father sold it to me on his deathbed,' said the Cavan man, 'and I gave him a cheque for it.'

☺ ☺ ☺

How do you know if you are in a Cavan supermarket?

Look for the rolls of brown toilet paper.

☺ ☺ ☺

A Cavan man has come up with a great way of getting round the huge charges that phone sex chat lines demand. He rings up the Samaritans and says, 'Talk dirty, or I'll top myself.'

☺ ☺ ☺

A Cavan man's wife died, so he went into a newspaper office to have a death notice inserted in the paper.

'Could I put in "Olga O'Reilly dead"?' he asked.

'Certainly sir,' said the clerk, 'it is €1 per word, but there is a minimum of six words.'

'Right,' said the Cavan man, 'I'll put "Olga O'Reilly dead. Hay for sale."'

☺ ☺ ☺

A Cavan man invited some friends to dinner in his house (don't laugh – it could happen!).

They commented on how nice his potatoes tasted.

'I grow them myself,' he said proudly.

'But you have no land, no garden, not even a window box,' said one of his friends.

'That's true right enough,' said the Cavan man, 'but do you remember meself and the wife bought a burial plot a few years ago for when the time comes for us to go? In the meantime isn't it a grand place to grow a few spuds.'

☺ ☺ ☺

A Cavan man won ten million euro in the Lotto and his wife said, 'There'll be no need for the old scrubbing brush any more.'

'No,' smiled the Cavan man, 'you can buy a new one now.'

Where did the idea for limbo dancing come from?

Some fellow was watching a Cavan man getting into a pay toilet for free.

☺ ☺ ☺

What is a Cavan child's fondest memory?

The night the tooth-fairy left an IOU.

☺ ☺ ☺

A Cavan man sent a letter to the newspapers: 'If you print any more offensive jokes about Cavan men,' he wrote, 'I will stop borrowing your publication.'

☺ ☺ ☺

A little Cavan boy was out with his father one day when he heard the chimes of the ice cream van.

'Can I have an ice cream please Dad?' he asked.

'Son,' said the Cavan man, 'the man in the ice cream van plays that music only when he has run out of ice cream.'

☺ ☺ ☺

How do you know if you are flying over Cavan?

Toilet paper on the clothes line.

☺ ☺ ☺

Cavan men have a great reputation for being romantic. Whenever you see a Cavan man walking in public with his wife, he is sure to be holding her hand. That's because if he lets go she'll start shopping.

A Cavan man emigrated to the United States but when he arrived home after thirty years he hardly recognised any of his three brothers. Each had a beard down to his waist.

'Why the beards, brothers?' he asked.

'Well,' said one of them, 'you took the razor to America with you.'

☺   ☺   ☺

A Cavan man read in the newspapers that a child in Africa lives on ten cents a day. So he sent all his kids to Africa.

☺   ☺   ☺

A beggar man knocked on a Cavan man's door and said, 'I haven't touched a mouthful of food in over a week.'

'Holy God,' said the Cavan man, 'I wish I had your willpower.'

☺   ☺   ☺

A Cavan man had five daughters and by the time the fifth one got married the confetti was filthy.

☺   ☺   ☺

A Cavan man got down on one knee to propose to his lady love, when a ten-cent piece fell out of his pocket and rolled under the sofa. By the time he emerged from under the sofa with the coin triumphantly between his teeth, the girl had lost interest.

☺ ☺ ☺

A Cavan man arrived home and handed his wife a big bunch of flowers.

'How romantic,' she sighed.

'Don't get too excited now,' said the Cavan man, 'I found them on the bus.'

☺ ☺ ☺

A Cavan man went into a clothes shop and said to the assistant, 'I'd like to see the cheapest suit in the shop.'

'You're wearing it sir,' said the assistant.

☺ ☺ ☺

A Cavan man was in the Social Welfare Office and stated on his application form that he was married.

'Where is your wedding ring then?' asked the clerk.

'The wife is wearing it this week,' said the Cavan man.

☺ ☺ ☺

A Cavan man in a restaurant dropped a ten-cent coin under the table. So he said to the waiter, 'If you find it, give it to me; if not, you can have it as a tip.'

☺   ☺   ☺

A Cavan man was sitting in the middle of the town square on a very cold night when a policeman asked him what he was doing.

'I spilled a bottle of beer,' the Cavan man told him, 'and I'm waiting for it to freeze so I can take it home with me.'

☺   ☺   ☺

Cavan men never have their clothes dry-cleaned. They donate them to charity shops and buy them back when they've been cleaned.

☺   ☺   ☺

A Cavan man gave his wife a mink outfit for her birthday – a trap and a shotgun.

☺   ☺   ☺

A Cavan man was very sick with a highly contagious disease.

'Send in my creditors,' he said to his wife, 'at last I can give each of them something.'

☺   ☺   ☺

How do you recognise a Cavan Santa Claus?

He comes down the chimney and sells the kids good toys cheaply.

☺   ☺   ☺

How does a Cavan man file his toenails?

Under 'T'.

☺   ☺   ☺

A Cavan man in a pub accidentally dropped a two-cent coin down a filthy toilet.

'Leave it,' said his friend, but the Cavan man immediately threw a €2 coin down the same toilet.

'Why the hell did you do that?' asked the friend.

'I'm not putting my hand down there just for two cent,' said the Cavan man.

☺   ☺   ☺

A little Cavan lad was doing a science examination. One of the questions was: what is the difference between lightning and electricity?

He wrote: 'You have to pay for electricity.'

☺   ☺   ☺

A Cavan man and his wife were having a disagreement.

'I'll have you know,' she shouted, 'if it weren't for my money, this house would not be here at all.'

'And I'll have you know,' the Cavan man retorted, 'if it weren't for your money, I wouldn't be here either.'

☺ ☺ ☺

A Cavan man came home from work unexpectedly at lunchtime and found a plumber's van parked outside his house.

'I hope to God,' he said to himself, 'that the wife is having an affair.'

☺ ☺ ☺

Why did a Cavan man refuse to pay his water rates?

He reckoned it would keep the water out of his house during the floods.

☺ ☺ ☺

How do you recognise a Cavan man's will?

He leaves everything to himself.

☺ ☺ ☺

A firm offered a prize of €100 for the best money-saving idea.

The prize went to a Cavan man who suggested that the prize be cut to €20.

☺ ☺ ☺

A Cavan man was chatting up a girl at a party. He said to her, 'Didn't I hear vaguely somewhere that your father died and left you €10,938,401 and 73 cent?'

☺ ☺ ☺

How was the jigsaw puzzle invented?
A Cavan man accidentally dropped a bank-note into a shredding machine.

☺ ☺ ☺

When a Cavan man died there was no problem winding up his estate. All he left was a clock.

☺ ☺ ☺

A Cavan man was stopped by a beggar who told him he had not eaten a square meal in days. The Cavan man gave him an OXO cube.

☺ ☺ ☺

A travelling salesman knocked at a Cavan man's door and asked him if he was interested in buying a dishwasher.
'Not at all,' said the Cavan man, 'sure haven't I got the best dishwasher in the country – the wife.'

☺ ☺ ☺

How much does a Cavan man pay for an engage-ment ring?
Half.

☺ ☺ ☺

A Cavan man in hospital was watching Mass on television one Sunday morning. When the collection plate was being passed around he changed channels.

☺ ☺ ☺

A customer asked a Cavan shopkeeper why there were so many misspelled and ungrammatical notices in his shop window.

The Cavan man smiled, 'Everyone thinks I'm a stupid uneducated fool and comes into the shop to cheat me. Business is booming.'

☺ ☺ ☺

There was a psychiatrist who treated only schizo-phrenics so he could send each one of them two bills every month.

One day a Cavan patient came in to his office. After a thorough examination, the psychiatrist said, 'That will be €200 please.'

'Here's €100,' said the Cavan man, 'the other fellow can look after himself.'

☺ ☺ ☺

A Cavan teacher was warning her pupils about the necessity of wrapping up well in the cold weather.

'A little boy I knew,' she warned them, 'went out on his sled in the snow without a coat, gloves or a hat, caught a chill and died.'

There was a stunned silence, broken only by a voice asking, 'Where's his sled, Miss?'

☺ ☺ ☺

Have you heard what the Cavan man bought his wife for her birthday?

A pre-electric toothbrush. 'You just hold it steady,' he told her, 'and move your head up and down.'

☺ ☺ ☺

'You haven't left me a tip,' said a waitress to a Cavan man. 'Why even the world's champion miser once left me a tip of ten cent.'

'Meet the new world champion,' said the Cavan man.

☺ ☺ ☺

How do you know if you are in a Cavan taxi?

The meter goes faster than the cab.

☺ ☺ ☺

A Cavan man was out driving one day when he was flagged down by a woman who shouted that she had just run out of petrol.

'Can you help me?' she asked.

'Certainly,' said the Cavan man, 'I have a full tank, follow me to the nearest filling station.'

☺ ☺ ☺

A Cavan man had the world's most faithful dog. He sold him six times and the dog always came back home again.

☺   ☺   ☺

One Cavan man was telling another about how a mutual friend of theirs had gone to watch the Cavan football team play a match in Croke Park and had dropped dead going into the match.

'Did he drop dead before or after he bought his ticket?' the first asked.

'After he bought it,' said the second.

'That was a terrible tragedy altogether,' said the first Cavan man.

☺   ☺   ☺

'Look,' said a Cavan man to his bank manager, 'if you are going to make such a fuss about my overdraft, I will withdraw it and take it to another bank where it will be appreciated.'

☺   ☺   ☺

A Cavan beggar man sat on the street displaying the following notice:

SPECIAL OFFER TODAY
GIVE JUST 50% OF WHAT YOU
NORMALLY GIVE

☺   ☺   ☺

What do Cavan men often part with?

A comb!

☺   ☺   ☺

Have you heard about the Cavan bank robber who was picked up by the police?

He went into a bank, demanded €100,000 and when the teller gave it to him, he stopped to count it.

☺   ☺   ☺

A Cavan gambler was asked how he managed to make a lot of money playing cards, but seemed to have no luck when it came to betting on horses.

'Maybe,' he smiled, 'it is because they won't let me shuffle the horses.'

☺   ☺   ☺

A Cavan man's wife asked him to take her somewhere really expensive for her birthday. He took her to his local petrol station.

☺   ☺   ☺

A Cavan man's wife was complaining about the state of her only coat.

'Look at it,' she said to him, 'there isn't a single button left on it. I'm ashamed to be seen wearing it.'

'OK,' said the Cavan man, 'tomorrow we are going shopping together.'

'For a new coat?' she squealed excitedly.

'No,' said the Cavan man, 'for buttons.'

☺   ☺   ☺

You've got to hand it to a Cavan man – otherwise he'll never pick up the bill.

☺   ☺   ☺

A Cavan man approached the desk in a big hotel.

'How much for a room?' he asked.

'€60 for a room on the ground floor,' said the clerk, '€50 for rooms on the first floor, €40 for rooms on the second floor, €30 for rooms on the third floor, and €20 for rooms on the top fourth floor.'

As the Cavan man turned to leave, the clerk said, 'What's the matter? Are our prices too dear for you?'

'No,' said the Cavan man, 'your hotel isn't tall enough for me.'

☺   ☺   ☺

A Cavan man proposed to his girlfriend and to his delight, she accepted.

'Do you mind,' she asked him, 'if I carry on with my job after we are married?'

'Mind?' said the Cavan man. 'I'm depending on it.'

☺   ☺   ☺

A Cavan man went into a grocer's shop and asked for six eggs laid by a black hen.

'I don't know the difference between eggs laid by hens of different colours,' said the grocer. 'Pick them out for yourself.'

So the Cavan man picked out the six biggest eggs he could find in the shop, paid for them and walked out smiling.

☺   ☺   ☺

A Cavan man on a bus journey to Dublin got off and on the bus at every stop.

He explained, 'If a ticket inspector turns up, I can always say truthfully, that I got on at the last stop.'

☺   ☺   ☺

A Cavan man found an unopened pay packet on the street so he went into a bar to have a drink.

'I believe you had some good luck finding some money,' said the barman, 'so why are you sitting there with such a long face?'

'Look at the amount of tax they deducted,' groaned the Cavan man.

☺   ☺   ☺

Teacher: If your father borrowed €1,000 to be paid back at €100 a month, how much would he owe after six months?

Cavan boy: €1,000, teacher.
Teacher: You don't know your sums boy.
Cavan boy: And you don't know my father, teacher.

☺   ☺   ☺

Have you heard about the Cavan man who submitted an income tax form claiming depreciation on his wife?

☺   ☺   ☺

Two Cavan men arrive in hell to find it covered in snow, ice, frost and a temperature of minus ten degrees centigrade.

'What the hell is going on?' one asked the other.

'I can only conclude,' said his friend, 'that Cavan have just won the All-Ireland Senior Football Championship.'

☺   ☺   ☺

A Cavan man's wife had her credit card stolen, but he didn't report it because whoever had taken it was spending a lot less than she would have.

☺   ☺   ☺

A Cavan publican picked up the phone in his bar one night and was told there was a terrorist bomb on the premises.

'Last orders there, gents please,' he shouted.

☺   ☺   ☺

A Cavan man won €10,000,000 in the Lotto. His wife asked him what they were doing to do about the begging letters.

'Keep sending them out,' said the Cavan man. 'Keep sending them out!'

☺   ☺   ☺

A Cavan man was exploring deepest Africa when he fell into a crocodile-infested river. However, he survived without a scratch because he was wearing a T-shirt with the motto: CAVAN FOR THE SAM MAGUIRE CUP.

And not even the crocodiles would swallow that!

☺   ☺   ☺

A Cavan man's hobby was collecting supermarket shopping trollies.

'At just €1 each, I can't resist them,' he said.

☺   ☺   ☺

A Cavan preacher to his congregation: 'I don't mind you putting buttons in the collection plate, but please provide your own buttons and don't pull them off the church cushions.'

☺   ☺   ☺

A Cavan shopkeeper lay dying with this family gathered round him.

'Is my wife Mary there?' he asked.

'Yes, Mary is here.'

'Is my son Seán there?'

'Yes, Seán is here.'

'Is my daughter Bridget there?'

'Yes, Bridget is here.'

With his dying groan, the Cavan man said, 'Then who the hell is minding the shop?'

☺   ☺   ☺

A Cavan man went to his doctor and the doctor observed that the Cavan man's stutter seemed to have vanished almost completely.

'Yes,' said the Cavan man, 'I've had to phone America a lot recently.'

☺   ☺   ☺

An American tourist was lost in the Cavan countryside and wandered about for nearly a week. Finally, on the seventh day he met a local.

'Thank Heavens I've met you,' he cried, 'I've been lost for a week.'

'Is there a reward out for you?' asked the Cavan man.

'No,' said the American.

'Well you're still lost,' said the Cavan man.

☺   ☺   ☺

A Cavan man developed a nice money-making racket. Whenever he and his wife went out for an evening, they got the kids to do a song and a dance act for the baby-sitter and deducted a cover charge from her money.

☺   ☺   ☺

'A man lost a €1 coin this morning in the town,' said a Cavan man to his friend, 'and I couldn't move until the crowd dispersed.'

'Why couldn't you move?' asked the friend.

'Well,' said the Cavan man, 'I didn't want to take my foot off the €1 coin.'

☺   ☺   ☺

A Cavan man was sentenced to death by hanging and on learning that it would cost €1,000 to carry out the hanging, offered to shoot himself for €100.

☺   ☺   ☺

A Cavan woman asked her husband if he would buy her a barometer so she could forecast the weather.

'You don't need a barometer, woman,' he told her. 'What do you think the good Lord gave you rheumatism for?'

☺   ☺   ☺

A Cavan man had a severe heart problem, so he bought a wind-up pacemaker.

☺   ☺   ☺

A Cavan man thought his bank was in big trouble when all his cheques were returned marked 'insufficient funds'.

☺   ☺   ☺

A Cavan man once gave up reading the free newspapers at his local library because of the wear and tear on his glasses.

☺   ☺   ☺

How did they stop crime in Cavan?

By putting the following notice over the jailhouse:

ANYBODY CONVICTED AND PUT
IN JAIL WILL HAVE TO PAY FOR HIS
BOARD AND LODGING

☺   ☺   ☺

A Cavan man's wife asked him to buy her a run-about as a present. So he bought her a tracksuit.

☺   ☺   ☺

'My girlfriend has just lost all her money in the bank crash,' said a Cavan man to a friend.

'You must feel very sorry for her,' said the friend.

'Indeed, I do,' said the Cavan man, 'and I'm going to miss her terribly.'

☺   ☺   ☺

A beggar stopped a Cavan man in the street and asked him for fifty cent for a cup of coffee.

'Show me the cup of coffee first,' said the Cavan man.

☺   ☺   ☺

A Cavan man in a queue at a bank developed a very severe case of hiccups.

'Could you – hic – tell me – hic – the balance – hic – in my account – hic – please,' he asked the cashier.

'You are €100,000 overdrawn,' said the cashier.

'You must be joking!' said the Cavan man.

'I am sir, but it certainly cured your hiccups, didn't it?'

☺   ☺   ☺

A Cavan man was travelling by rail in the United States of America. He asked the railway clerk for a ticket to Springfield.

'Which Springfield, Mister?' asked the clerk, 'Missouri, Ohio, Illinois or Massachusetts?'

'Which one is the cheapest?' asked the Cavan man.

☺   ☺   ☺

The following note was pinned to a fire alarm in a Cavan factory:

IN CASE OF FIRE
KEEP IT TO YOURSELF
OR EVERYONE WILL WANT ONE

☺   ☺   ☺

A middle-aged Cavan man has a whole room full of children's toys in his house. He never threw an item away.

He's keeping them for his second childhood.

☺   ☺   ☺

A Cavan man was taking his girlfriend for a drive on his motorbike. As they passed a hotdog stand she sighed, 'My, those hotdogs smell nice.'

'Hold on a moment,' said the Cavan man, 'I'll drive a little closer to the stand so you can get a better smell.'

☺   ☺   ☺

A Cavan man told a friend that his wife was always asking for money.

'Last month it was €500, last week it was €700, and yesterday it was €600,' he told him.

'And what does she do with all the money?' the friend asked.

'Nothing,' said the Cavan man, 'I never give her any.'

☺   ☺   ☺

A Cavan man kept vigil at the bedside of his dying wife for several days. Finally he said, 'Mary, I must be off on business now, but I'll hurry back. And if you feel yourself slipping away while I'm gone, would you mind blowing out the candle?'

☺   ☺   ☺

'Mammy,' said a little Cavan lad to his mother, 'can I please have €1 for a man outside who's crying?'

'Certainly,' said the mother, handing over the money. 'What is he crying about?'

'He's crying "ice cream, ice cream, ice cream",' shouted the true son of Cavan.

☺   ☺   ☺

How do we know there was a Cavan man at the last supper?

Someone asked for a separate cheque.

☺   ☺   ☺

A Cavan man went to the doctor and said, 'Doc, you've got to help me – I've swallowed a €1 coin.'

'When did this happen?' the doctor asked.

'About two years ago,' said the Cavan man.

'Why have you delayed so long coming to see me?' asked the doctor.

'Well, I didn't really need the money until now.'

☺   ☺   ☺

An old Cavan man lay dying, surrounded by his family and wife.

'O'Reilly owes me €1,000,' he moaned.

'Listen to that,' said the wife, 'coherent to the last.'

'O'Donnell owes me €800,' he groaned.

'Still of sound mind,' smiled the wife.

'I owe O'Neill €2,000,' he mumbled.

'Listen to the man rave,' said the wife.

☺   ☺   ☺

A Cavan man asked a friend for a cigarette.

'I thought you'd given up smoking,' said the friend.

'Well,' said the Cavan man, 'I've accomplished phase one of quitting.'

'What's that?'

'I've stopped buying them.'

☺   ☺   ☺

A little Cavan lad showed his father a beautiful new golf ball that he had found.

'Are you sure it was lost son?' his father inquired.

'I'm sure dad, I even saw the man looking for it.'

☺   ☺   ☺

A Cavan man's wife was very sick so her doctor felt that some sea air might do her good.

One morning she woke to find her husband fanning her with a kipper.

☺ ☺ ☺

Have you heard about the Cavan criminal?

When they put a price on his head, he turned himself in.

☺ ☺ ☺

The first time a Cavan man discovered the free air machine at his local garage he blew out all four tyres.

☺ ☺ ☺

How do you recognise a house built by a Cavan builder?

There's no roof on the shower room.

☺ ☺ ☺

The wall round the cemetery in a Cavan town had fallen into disrepair so a committee was formed to help build a new one.

A door-to-door collection was organised, and a certain notoriously fiscally careful Cavan man was approached for a contribution.

'There's no need for that wall at all,' he told the collectors. 'People outside don't want to go in and those inside can't get out.'

☺ ☺ ☺

Sign in a Cavan office:

THERE IS NO SUCH THING AS PETTY CASH

☺   ☺   ☺

How does a Cavan man have a bubble bath?
He has a tin of baked beans for dinner.

☺   ☺   ☺

A Cavan man and a Donegal man went on a motoring trip together and decided to share expenses. The Donegal man bought the petrol and the oil while the Cavan man looked after the water and the air for the tyres.

☺   ☺   ☺

A Cavan man emigrated to New York where he set up as a shoeshine boy. But even here his native cunning did not desert him. He had the following notice on his street stall:

ONE SHOE SHINED ABSOLUTELY FREE

☺   ☺   ☺

A Cavan man went into a grocer's shop to buy some eggs.

'How much are the eggs?' he asked the assistant.

'€5 a dozen for the whole ones,' said the assistant, 'but €3 a dozen for the cracked ones.'

'Right,' said the Cavan man, 'crack me a dozen.'

☺   ☺   ☺

A Cavan man was in a pub when a fly fell into his beer. So he lifted the fly up carefully by the wings and held it above the glass.

'Now you little devil,' he said to it, 'spit it out or I'll squeeze it out of you.'

☺   ☺   ☺

A Cavan man made the mistake of consulting a Cavan lawyer with a reputation of running a very sharp practice.

'Is it true,' asked the Cavan man, 'that you charge €500 for answering three questions?'

'That's true,' said the lawyer.

'Isn't that a bit expensive?' asked the Cavan man.

'Not when you consider my years of training,' said the lawyer. 'Now what's your third question?'

☺   ☺   ☺

A Cavan man suddenly came into contact with dozens of long lost relatives, but he wasn't pleased. He had just won the lottery.

☺   ☺   ☺

A Cavan businessman was approached by an insurance agent asking him if he would like to take out a policy covering fire and flood on his premises.

'Fire I know about,' said the Cavan man, 'but how the hell do you start a flood?'

☺ ☺ ☺

A Cavan man saw a really good offer on television with cash available to people prepared to change their bank.

One question on the application form asked: Name of previous bank?

The Cavan man wrote: Piggy.

☺ ☺ ☺

A Cavan woman went to her husband and said she wanted a new dress.

'What's wrong with the one you've got?' he asked her.

'Well,' she told him, 'it's too long and I can't do the housework because the veil keeps falling in my eyes.'

☺ ☺ ☺

A Cavan man said to his wife, 'Do you remember always saying to me that you would like to live in a more expensive house?'

'Yes,' said the wife excitedly.

'Well,' said the Cavan man, 'your dream has come true – our landlord has raised the rent.'

☺　☺　☺

A Cavan man's wife was fishing when she fell into the river.

'Help, save me,' she shouted, 'I'm drowning.'

The Cavan man rushed to the bank and drew all the money out of their joint account.

☺　☺　☺

A Cavan man who went to live in Dublin went out of his way to be generous, standing drinks in his local pub to counteract all those stories about his fellow countymen.

When he was returning home to live in Cavan for good he was disgusted to find that all along his friends thought he was from Monaghan.

☺　☺　☺

Why did a Cavan man have a window in the front of his fridge?

So he could see if the little light went off.

☺　☺　☺

A Cavan man was feeling out of sorts so he went to the doctor who examined him thoroughly.

'I think you should give up drinking and smoking,' said the doctor.

The Cavan man said nothing but got up to leave the surgery.

'You haven't paid me for my advice,' said the doctor.

'No,' said the Cavan man, 'because I don't intend to take it.'

☺   ☺   ☺

A Cavan man was in hospital and had a big bowl of almonds beside his bed. Untypically he was offering them to all his visitors explaining, 'They were a funny present my brother bought me. I have no teeth at the moment but I was able to lick all the chocolate off them.'

☺   ☺   ☺

A beggar man came up to a Cavan man in the street and said, 'Can I tap you for a tenner?'

The Cavan man replied, 'Look, for a tenner you can knock me down and walk all over me.'

☺   ☺   ☺

A Cavan man was known locally as 'the Exorcist'. Every time he visited a house, all the spirits vanished.

☺   ☺   ☺

A Cavan man was on his deathbed writhing in agony. But his wife brought him back to reality saying to him, 'There's no need to wear out the sheets tossing and turning just because you're dying.'

☺ ☺ ☺

Household tip from a Cavan magazine: 'Increase the life of your carpets by rolling them up and keeping them in the garage.'

☺ ☺ ☺

Cavan people count the number of tourists in the county each year by the number of banknotes in the church collection plates.

☺ ☺ ☺

A Cavan man asked a bus conductor how much it would cost to travel into town.

'€1,' said the conductor, so the Cavan man decided to run behind the bus for five stops.

'How much now?' he asked the conductor.

'€2,' said the conductor. 'You're running in the wrong direction.'

☺ ☺ ☺

A Cavan man invited his girlfriend home to a candlelight supper.

His fuse had blown.

☺ ☺ ☺

A delivery man brought a new computer to a Cavan man's house and the Cavan man handed him a cheque for €1,000.

'Are you allowed to accept a tip?' asked the Cavan man.

'I am, sir,' said the delivery man.

'Well don't try to cash the cheque,' said the Cavan man.

☺   ☺   ☺

For their 39th wedding anniversary, a Cavan man bought his wife a gravestone.

For their 40th wedding anniversary, she asked him if he was going to buy her a special present.

'No,' he said, 'you haven't used the present I bought you last year yet.'

☺   ☺   ☺

A Cavan man proposed to his girlfriend and was accepted.

'Now that we are engaged,' she said to him, 'I'd like you to give me a ring.'

'Certainly,' said the Cavan man, 'what's your number?'

☺   ☺   ☺

A Cavan man took his girlfriend out to dinner but during the first course discovered a fly in his soup. So he kicked up such a fuss that the manager offered the two of them dinner on the house which they enjoyed immensely.

Then they moved to a café next door and the Cavan man said, 'Would you like a dessert? I have one fly left.'

☺   ☺   ☺

A Cavan man was experiencing financial diffi-culties so he gathered his six children around him and told them, 'Times is hard kids. I'm going to have to let two of ye go.'

☺   ☺   ☺

A Cavan man took his wife on a blowout trip to Belfast. They went into a café and he ordered a cup of tea and two saucers.

☺   ☺   ☺

A Cavan man asked a friend for the loan of €100.
'I have only got €50,' said the friend.
'That's OK,' said the Cavan man, 'you can owe me €50, I'll owe you €50 and we'll be quits.'

☺   ☺   ☺

How do you recognise a Cavan man in a restau-rant?
He reads the menu from right to left.

☺   ☺   ☺

A Cavan man went skiing in the Alps but got lost and lay all night freezing in the snow. In the morning a rescue worker reached him and shouted, 'I'm from the Red Cross.'

'I gave at the office,' said the Cavan man.

☺   ☺   ☺

A shout went up at a Cavan bank: 'Did anyone lose a roll of banknotes with a rubber band around them?'

'Yes, yes,' came several voices, 'I did.'

'Well I just found a rubber band.'

☺   ☺   ☺

A Cavan man stood before the Pearly Gates of Heaven.

'You have to pass a test before you can get in,' said Saint Peter. 'Take this leaky bucket and empty Lough Erne.'

'My, that's an awful lot of water,' said the Cavan man. 'Isn't there any other test I can take?'

'Well,' said Saint Peter, 'you could stand at the bar of a Cavan pub until someone offers you a free drink.'

'Give us a look at that aul bucket again,' said the Cavan man.

☺   ☺   ☺

The fellow who invented slow-motion films got

the idea while watching a Cavan man reach for a bill at a restaurant.

☺   ☺   ☺

A Cavan man received the following letter from his local undertaker:

Dear Sir,
If you do not pay the final instalment on your mother-in-law's funeral, UP SHE COMES!

☺   ☺   ☺

We don't rightly know where golf was invented, but it certainly wasn't Cavan. No Cavan man would have invented a game in which a ball could be lost.

☺   ☺   ☺

A beggar man stopped a Cavan man in the street and asked for a little help. The Cavan man dipped deeply into his pocket and produced a two-cent piece which he handed over.

'And how did you get into this unfortunate position?' he asked him.

'Like yourself sir,' said the beggar man, 'I was always giving away vast sums of money to the poor and needy.'

☺   ☺   ☺

A Cavan man's car broke down from lack of petrol so a passer-by offered to push him to a filling station. When they reached a filling station the Cavan man said, 'Would you mind pushing me to the next one please? This crowd give you very few points on the loyalty card.'

☺   ☺   ☺

A Cavan couple invited some people round to dinner and the husband immediately started to hide the umbrellas from the hall stand.

'There's no need to do that love,' said his wife, 'all our guests are completely honest and won't steal our umbrellas.'

'I'm not worried they'll steal them,' said the Cavan man, 'I'm just worried they'll recognise them.'

☺   ☺   ☺

A Cavan man went to the dentist and as he sat in the chair began to count his money.

'You don't have to pay me yet,' said the dentist.

'I'm just checking it before you put me under the anaesthetic,' said the Cavan man.

☺   ☺   ☺

Eulogy for a Cavan man: He was a man of rare gifts.

☺   ☺   ☺

A fellow met a Cavan man walking along the road wearing only one shoe.

'Have you lost a shoe?' he asked him.

'No,' said the Cavan man, 'I've just found one.'

☺ ☺ ☺

A Cavan man took his little son out to dinner in a hotel. After the meal the Cavan man asked the waiter for a doggy bag so he could take home the remains of the meal.

'Great,' said his son, 'are we getting a dog?'

☺ ☺ ☺

What is a Cavan man's greatest predicament? To find himself in church with only a €20 note on him.

☺ ☺ ☺

A Cavan man was mugged one night by two thugs and put up a tremendous fight before they subdued him. All they found in his pockets was a €1 coin.

'It's a good thing he didn't have €2,' said one of the thugs, 'or he'd have killed us both.'

☺ ☺ ☺

A Cavan farmer fell into a deep well. So he splashed about and called his wife for help.

'Hold on,' cried the wife, 'I'll call your labourers in from the fields to rescue you.'

'Wait,' said the Cavan man, 'what time is it?'

'Twelve thirty,' said his wife.

'Wait another half an hour,' said the Cavan man, 'I can swim around until lunchtime.'

☺   ☺   ☺

Two Cavan men met on the main street.

'How's the world treating you?' one asked.

'Very seldom,' replied the other, 'very seldom.'

☺   ☺   ☺

A Cavan man took his children to the seaside and bought them an ice-cream. But they weren't pleased because they wanted one each.

☺   ☺   ☺

'Do you believe in free speech?' a Cavan man asked a total stranger in the street.

'I do,' was the reply.

'In that case,' said the Cavan man, 'can I use your mobile phone?'

☺   ☺   ☺

In a rush of blood to the head, a Cavan man once gave a waiter a tip of €5.

'What are you going to spend it on?' he asked.

'I'm not going to spend it,' said the waiter, 'I'm going to have it framed and displayed on the wall, because no Cavan man ever left me a tip before.'

'In that case,' said the Cavan man, 'could you give it back to me and I'll give you a cheque?'

☺   ☺   ☺

A Cavan man had a big sign on his shop:

MONEY BACK IF NOT SATISFIED

When a customer came in demanding a refund, the Cavan man told him, 'Nothing doing – I'm quite satisfied.'

☺   ☺   ☺

What is the difference between a pigeon and a Cavan man?

A pigeon is more likely to put a deposit on a new car.

☺   ☺   ☺

What does a Cavan man do when it's cold?

He sits beside a candle.

What does a Cavan man do when it's absolutely freezing?

He lights the candle.

☺   ☺   ☺

A Cavan man awoke at 4 a.m. feeling very sick so he rang his doctor.

'How much do you charge for a house call?' he asked him.

'And how much for an office call?'

'€40,' said the doctor wearily.

'Right, doc,' said the Cavan man, 'I'll see you at your office in ten minutes.'

☺   ☺   ☺

'Will you marry me?' a Cavan man asked his girl-friend.

'But you've only known me for a few weeks,' said the girl.

'Maybe so,' said the Cavan man, 'but I've worked in the bank where your father keeps his money for over two years.'

☺   ☺   ☺

Sign in a Cavan restaurant:

PRICES MAY CHANGE BETWEEN COURSES

☺   ☺   ☺

A Cavan hotel doorman can open a taxi door for you with one hand, carry your bag in another hand and still have a hand free to receive a tip.

☺   ☺   ☺

The following is a true story, related to me by the greatest of Irish comedians, Doctor Niall Toibin, the man credited with the invention of the Cavan man joke: 'The parish priest in a certain Cavan town was appealing at Mass one Sunday for funds for the building of a new church. He addressed his congregation as follows: "It has come to my notice that certain comedians and joke book writers have been suggesting that Cavan people are not quite as generous as the inhabitants of other counties. Now I want you to nail that suggestion this morning for the lie that it undoubtedly is and dig deeply into your pockets for the new church fund. Put the matter beyond all doubt once and for all."'

Could you be up to them?

☺   ☺   ☺

A Cavan girl said to her boyfriend on a date, 'A penny for your thoughts.'

'I was thinking,' said the Cavan man, 'how nice it would be to give you a long kiss.'

So they had a good long kiss, then the Cavan man said, 'Now, how about that penny you owe me?'

☺   ☺   ☺

A Cavan man took his wife out and they had tea and biscuits. She wasn't very happy about having to give a pint of blood though.